LET'S START STILLWATER TROUT *FISHING*

Richard Willett

The Crowood Press

First published in 1990 by
The Crowood Press
Ramsbury, Marlborough,
Wiltshire SN8 2HE

British Library Cataloguing in Publication Data

Willett, Richard
Stillwater trout fishing.
1. Still waters. Trout. Angling.
I. Title
799.1'755

ISBN 1-85223-311-7

Typeset by Jahweh Associates, Stroud
Printed in Great Britain by MacLehose & Partners Ltd

Contents

Trout

There are two common trout species, the brown trout and the rainbow trout. The brown trout is native to Britain and Europe whilst the rainbow trout was introduced from America towards the end of the nineteenth century. Rainbow trout do not breed naturally in British lakes so stocks rely almost entirely on hatchery-reared fish. They can grow very large, sometimes up to thirty pounds in weight.

The name 'rainbow' implies a highly coloured fish, but in fact rainbow trout are often less colourful than brown trout. When in peak condition the rainbow trout is not very colourful at all, often having a silvery appearance. It

is when it approaches spawning condition that it takes on its true 'rainbow' colours. The male fish especially becomes very dark with a vivid red or pink band running along the length of its body. The spots on the rainbow are small and spread along the body of the fish, also covering the fins and tail.

The colouration of the brown trout can vary tremendously. Some brown trout are covered in spots while others only have a few spots on the gill covers and along the back. The spots on the brown trout are bigger than those on the rainbow and have a white or pale halo around them. Very few spots, if any, are found on the brown trout's tail.

Location

Trout are not a shoal fish although they may often be found feeding together in a reservoir.

In a large, featureless reservoir locating trout can be difficult. If a wind is blowing, it is best to fish into the wind. It will carry hatching insects to one side of the reservoir, and the trout will be in this area. It is not always easy casting into the wind but you should not have to cast far, since the trout will come in very close to the bank side.

When you are fishing from a boat on a reservoir, seek out the wind lanes. Wind blowing across the surface of a lake does not do so evenly. Small channels can be seen where the effect of the wind on the surface layer is greater. Most of the insect life will be carried to these wind lanes, so these are the places to find the trout.

open water can be explored by boat
old trees and undercuts – a good place to locate trout
brown trout
brown trout

far bank – trout close in
ast to trout that are rising
rainbow trout

Casting a Fly

It is important to understand that there is only one basic problem and therefore one real mistake to be made in fly casting. The problem is that you must make the fly rod do the work, and not your arm. The rod must be made to act as a spring to propel a virtually weightless object – the fly – through the air. The function of the spring is to store up energy, and then release it when required.

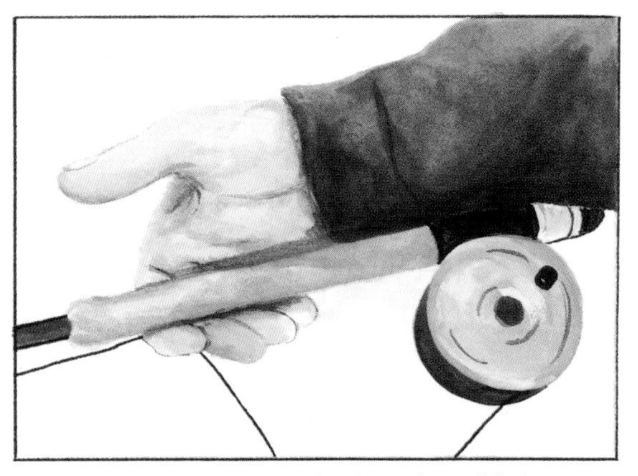

1. *The correct grip is vital – here the rod balances in the palm. Close the hand gently.*

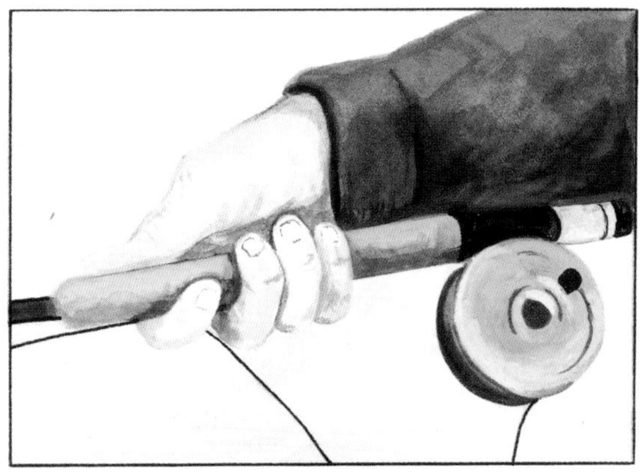

2. *The hand closed. The thumb along the top approach – light but firm.*

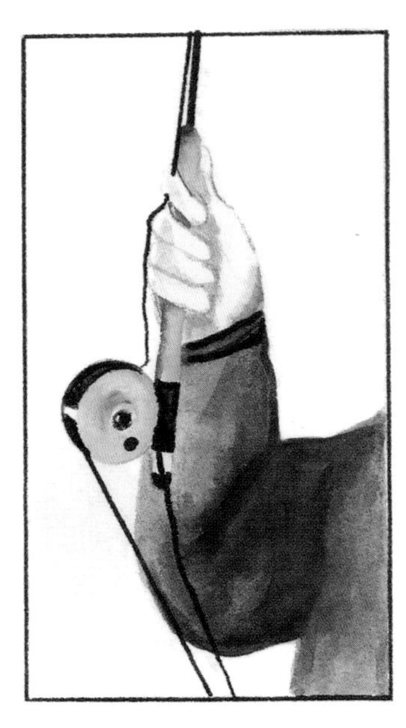

3. The wrist should not break past the vertical.

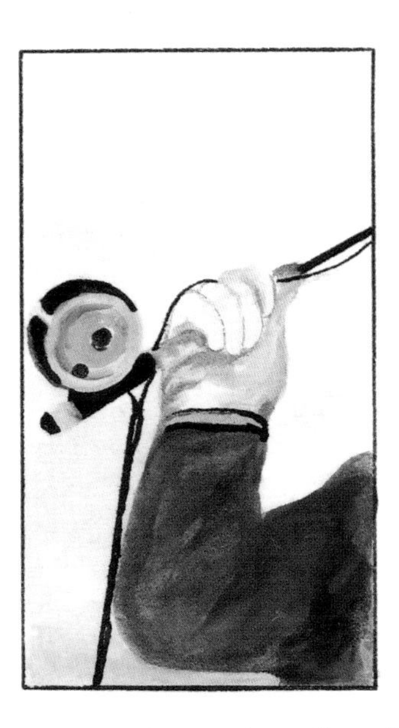

4. Here the wrist has collapsed, losing power and offering the chance of the line being caught up behind the angler.

5. Here the movement begins.

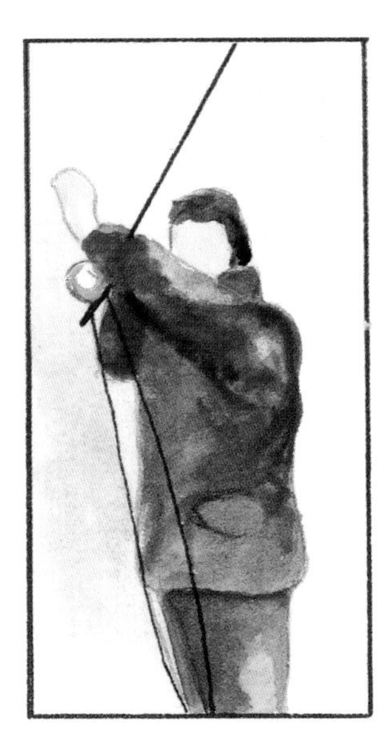

6. Accelerating into the cast. (9.30/10.00 to 12.00 position.)

7. The completed 'up' or 'back' cast; natural drift takes the rod back to the 12.30 to 1.00 position.

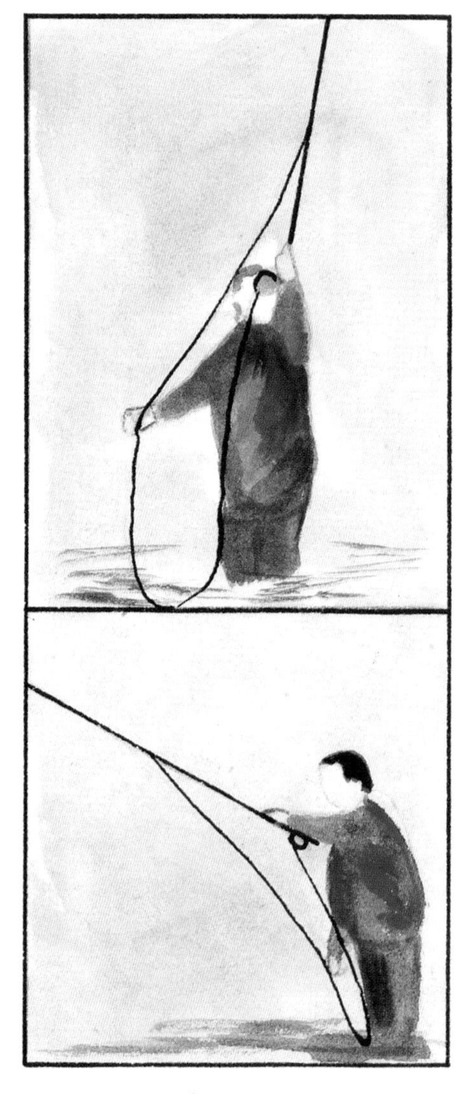

8. The forward cast begins.

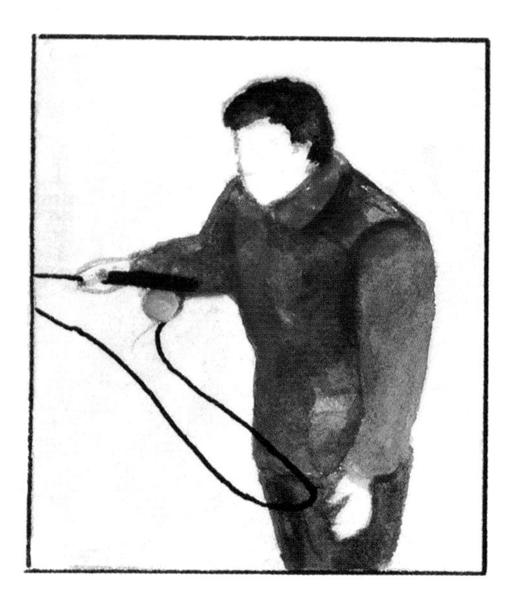

9. Maximum power is exerted forwards from the backcast and slightly downwards in trajectory.

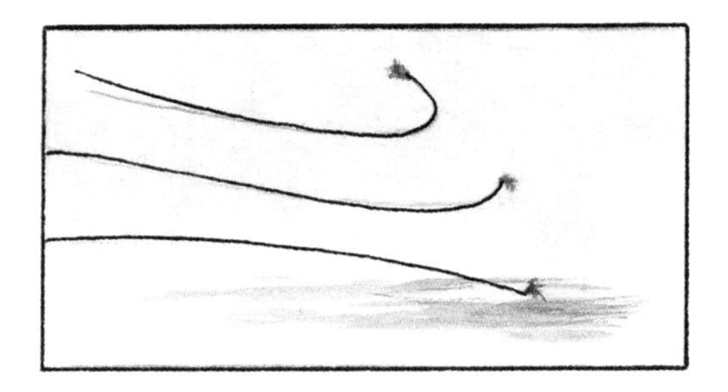

10. Release the line – et voilà!

Parts of a Fly

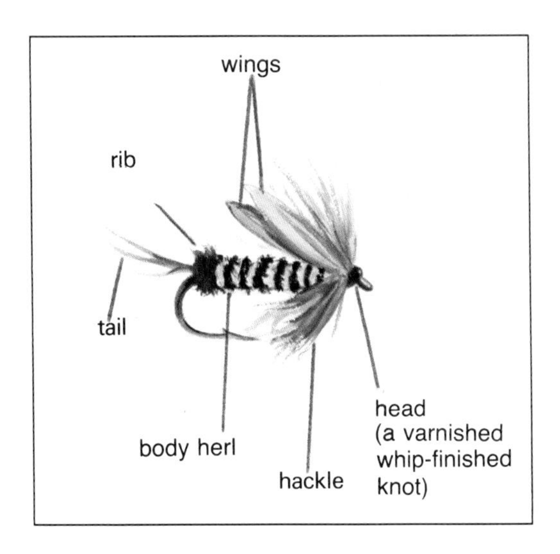

Trout Flies (General)

Fly-Fishing

Fly-fishing was once regarded as a superior method of catching fish. The skills of fly-fishing were greatly exaggerated, causing many anglers to be dissuaded from even attempting this method. Another thing which deterred anglers was that this form of fishing was mainly used to catch trout and grayling. In recent years, however, there has been a great upsurge in the popularity of fly-fishing and more people are now enjoying this fascinating side of the sport.

In my opinion, fly-fishing is a most enjoyable method of catching fish and is no more difficult to master than any other form of angling.

Basically, there are two main branches of fly-fishing. In one instnce the artificial fly is presented to the trout in such a way that it represents an insect which forms a major part of the trout's natural diet. The other form of fly-fishing is lure fishing, which is to present an artificial lure to the trout, representing a small fish. This is worked through the water so as to trigger off the natural predatory instinct of the fish, so that it grabs at the lure.

Whichever form of fly-fishing you decide to take up, the most important thing to do is to select a rod, reel and fly line that balance correctly. Not only will this enable you to cast with ease, but will save wear and tear on the tackle and also possible breakages. Rods and fly lines are marked with a number so that they can be easily matched together. The rods range from AFTM 3 to AFTM 12. This mark is printed on the rod next to the handle. AFTM simply stands for the Association of Fishing Tackle Makers – it is the number that is the most important. The lower the number the lighter and more delicate the rod. For our purpose, rods in the AFTM 5 to 7 range are ideal.

Some rods are designed to handle a number of lines while others will cope with only one. Make sure when you choose a rod that it feels comfortable with you and the reel. Make sure also that the balance of the tackle is just right.

Fly lines can be very expensive so learn to cast with a cheaper variety; you can graduate on to a better-quality line later. The size of line should be chosen to suit the rod and its AFTM rating. Several types of line are available and the novice should make sure he or she is buying the right one.

For delicate presentation of a fly and for general use there is the double-taper fly line. As the name implies, these lines are thickest in the centre and then taper at each end. These are usually represented as DT before the size number.

Weight-forward lines are self-explanatory and are used where distance casting is more important than delicate presentation. With practice, these can be cast delicately. They have the letters WF on them, then the size number. Floating fly lines are denoted by the letter F after the size number, and sinking lines by the letter S. The most versatile line for the beginner to choose for an AFTM 7 rod would be a DT 7 fly line.

Fly lines look clumsy but it must be remembered that it is the weight of the fly line which carries the fly to the fish. One advantage of using a double-taper fly line for small stillwater conditions is that, since it is rare to cast more than half the fly line when fishing, if one half begins to show signs of wear and tear the line can simply be reversed. Thus, two fly lines are bought for the price of one.

Fly lines are usually only 30 yards long so need some backing put on to the reel beneath them. It is unlikely that you will hook a fish that will take all the fly line off your reel but it is always best to be prepared. Braided backing can be bought from a tackle shop so make sure this is securely attached to your fly line.

A length of tapered nylon is attached to the hook end of the fly line; this is called a leader. It is this leader that presents your fly to the fish. Leaders are sold in 3-yard lengths, size coded Ox to 6x. This code denotes the diameter at the tip of the leader and the corresponding breaking strain. For example, Ox leaders have a breaking strain of 10 pounds and size 6x leaders have a breaking strain of 2 pounds. The higher the number the finer the point is. The leader tapers gradually from the loop which joins on to the fly line down to the fine point.

A short length of nylon line, called the point should be tied to the end of the leader with a Blood knot. The nylon line should be of the same breaking strain as the leader tip and should be about 18 inches long. The idea of tying a nylon point on the end of the leader is that every time you change the fly you reduce the length of the nylon line. If you tied a fly directly onto the nylon leader you would be working back towards and along the tapered length. After changing several flies you would have worked your way so far back along the tapered line that the point breaking strain would have increased, making the fly presentation rather clumsy.

Dry-Fly Fishing

One of the most enjoyable aspects of fly-fishing is that you can wander along the banks of a lake or reservoir without being weighted down by a lot of tackle. All you need is a box of flies and a few sundry items in a small trout bag. You can carry your rod and landing-net. Dry-fly fishing is to my mind one of the nicest ways of catching fish.

The nylon leader should be greased with silicon line grease to make it float, and whatever pattern of dry fly you decide to use should be dipped in fly floatant. Let the liquid dry for about a minute before casting and the fly will float for a considerable amount of time.

Dry-fly fishing is normally practised by casting up and across the lake, so that as the line drifts with the surface ripple, line can be drawn in with your spare hand so that you keep contact with the fly. Let the line that you draw back fall at your feet so that when you recast you can let it shoot out again, and don't have to pull line off the reel to cast again.

Selection of dry flies.

When you see a fish rising try to get fairly close to it without scaring it. Cast up to the fish so that the line does not come into its view. Cast about a yard in front of the trout so the fly sits in its path of vision. Don't put the fly right on top of its nose. When trout are stationed directly under the surface the rise will be a very gentle one as the trout sucks the fly under. Never be in too much of a hurry to drive the hook home and try to straighten up rather than to strike hard. Just hold the loose fly line with one hand and gently lift the rod with the other. Striking hard will possibly break the nylon point.

Wet-Fly Fishing

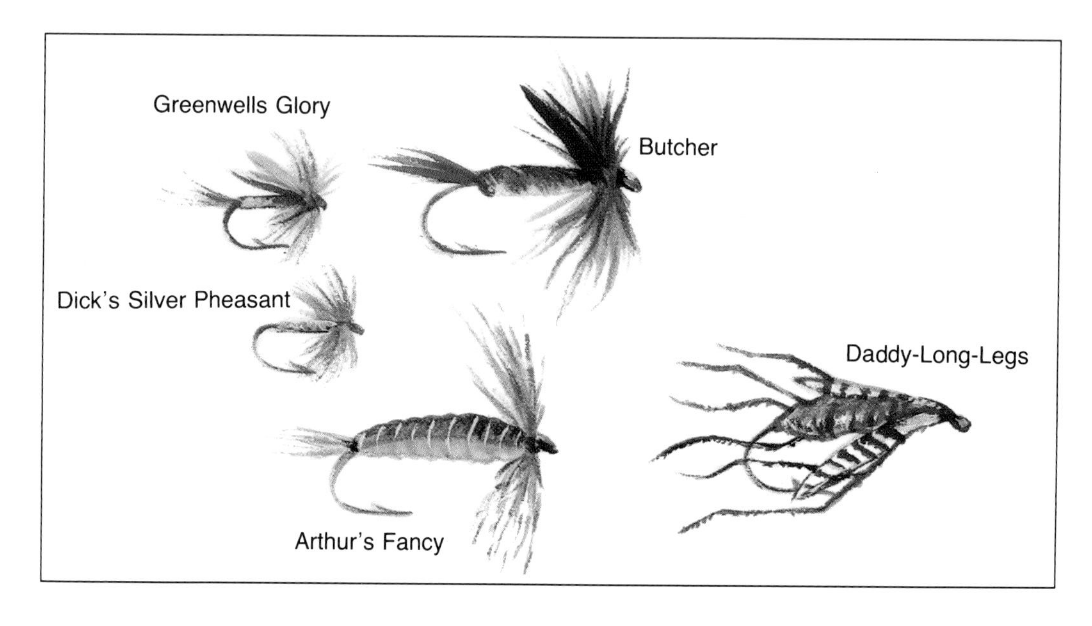

Selection of wet flies.

Wet-fly fishing calls for slightly different tactics to dry-fly fishing. The object of a wet fly is to imitate a drowned insect or the nymph stage of a fly that lives underwater. In most cases, a fly can be fished wet, still using a floating fly line. The nylon leader is 3 yards long and, if rubbed with a mixture of washing-up liquid and Fuller's earth, it will be degreased and sink. This length will get a fly down to most lake beds and reservoir margins.

When fishing lakes, the fly is cast out and the leader is allowed to sink. Very often it is while it is sinking that a trout will grab the fly. Once the fly has sunk it can be gently moved back towards the bank; this is done by drawing on the fly line. A fish taking the fly will move the line across the surface.

The type of fly you use depends on the water and the time of year. If an easily identified species of fly is hatching and the fish are feeding on this, then it would be common sense to use a pattern which imitates the insect. A general way of telling whether an artificial pattern should be fished wet or dry, is to look at the eye on the hook. A wet-fly hook has the eye turned down. Look after the flies you use and keep them stored properly.

Lure Fishing

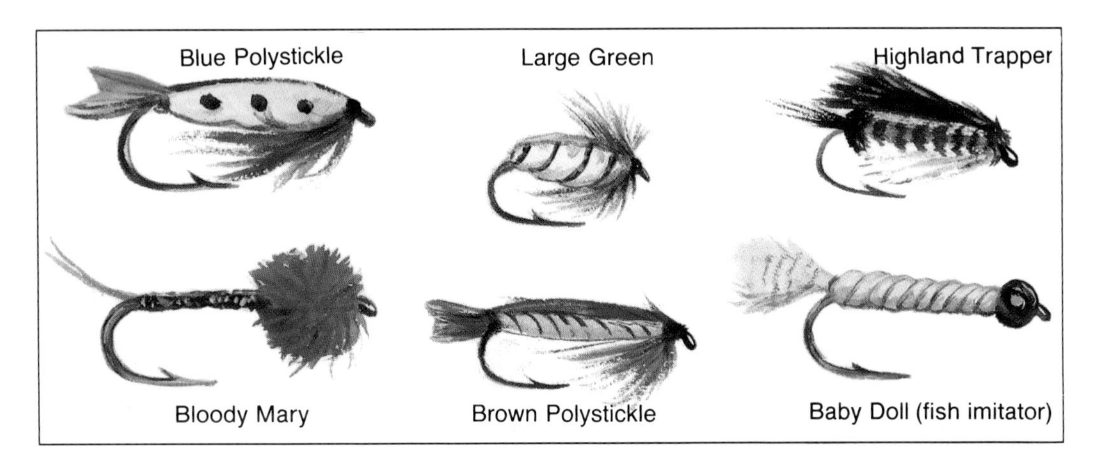

Reservoir lures.

Lure fishing is practised on lakes and big reservoirs and requires much stronger tackle since the conditions encountered on a reservoir are sometimes rough. On a large, open expanse of water the wind can whip the waves up to resemble an inland sea. The rod has to be powerful enough to punch a fly line out into the wind. Anglers wading in the margins disturb the fish so that on well-fished reservoirs long casting is needed.

The rod should be in the range of AFTM 7 to AFTM 9, with a line size to match. For lure, a beginner should use a weight-forward line and one which sinks to get the lure down to the fish. The nylon leader should also be a lot stronger than for normal fly-fishing.

The actual lures are tied to long-shank hooks and in the hand look quite pretty but unlike anything you find in the water. It is the movement through the water, given to lures by reeling in the line, which attracts the trout. The feathers and wool which form the lure are chosen for the colour patterns which, when moved underwater, resemble the colour and features of small fish. The line should be cast out into the reservoir and given plenty of time to sink. Keeping the rod tip pointing slightly down towards the water, strip back the line to work the lure back in towards you. Sometimes fish only react when the lure is stripped back at top speeds; at other times a fish will take a slowly retrieved lure.

Knots

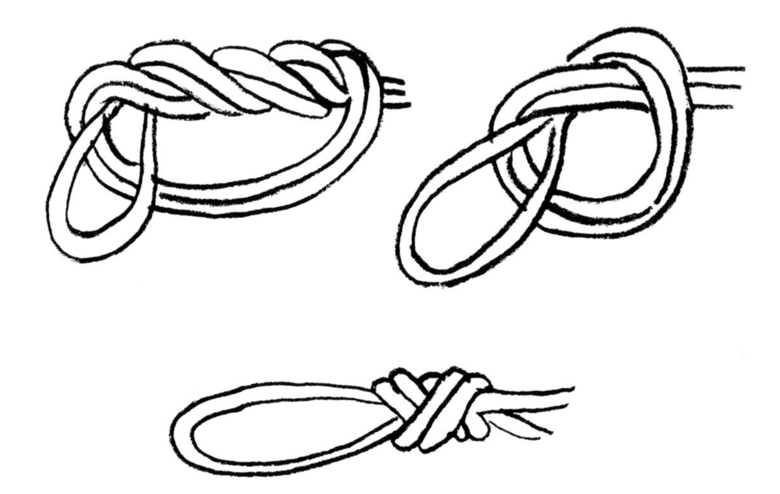

Three-turn Loop knot.

Method of joining hook length to reel line.

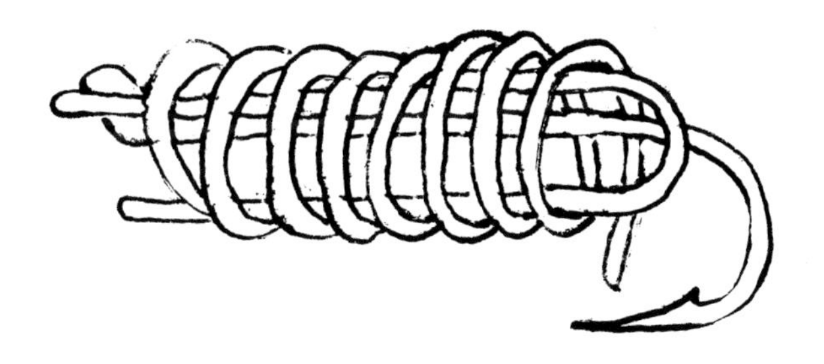

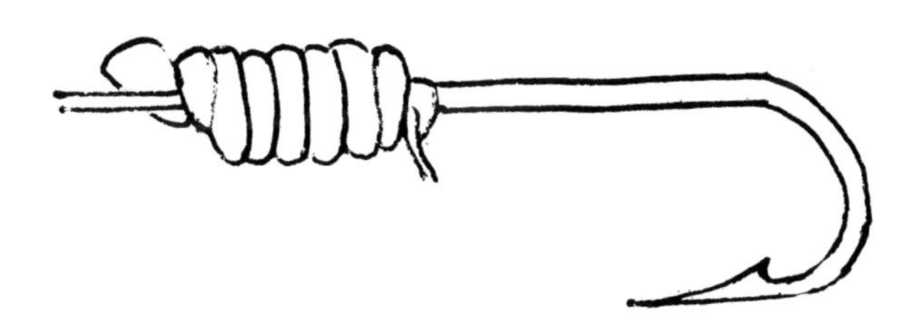

Spade End knot.

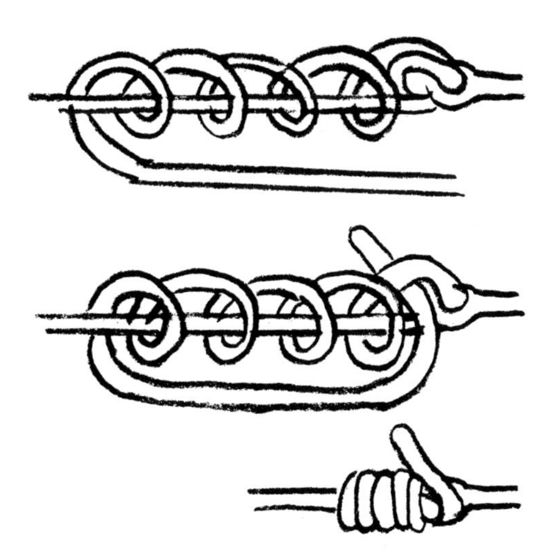

Clinch knot.

Leader Knots

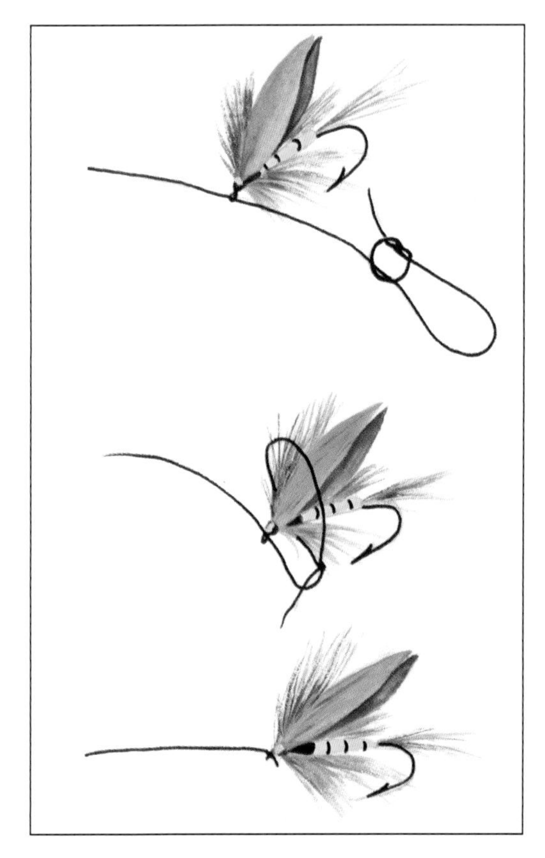

Single Turl knot. A useful knot for attaching flies to the cast. The Turl knot keeps the head of the fly in line with the nylon cast.

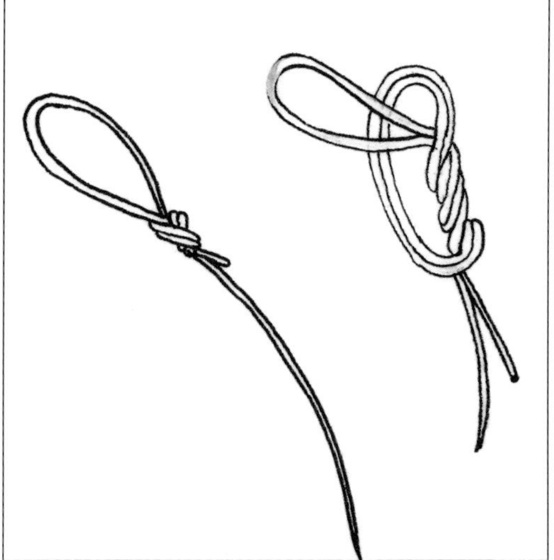

Overhand or Figure of Eight knot. Forms a loop in a hook snood or dropper.

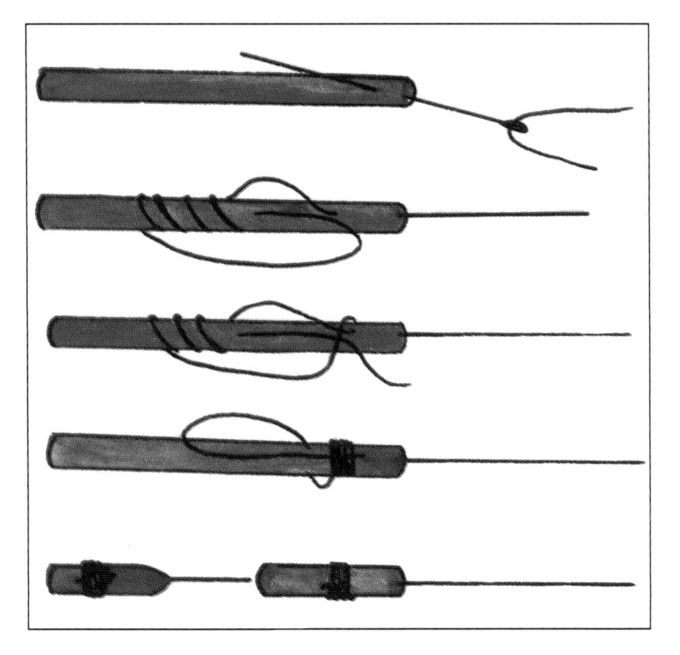

Grafham Pin knot. Joins a fly line to a permanent nylon leader. Casts are then tied to the nylon leader which preserves the fly line taper.

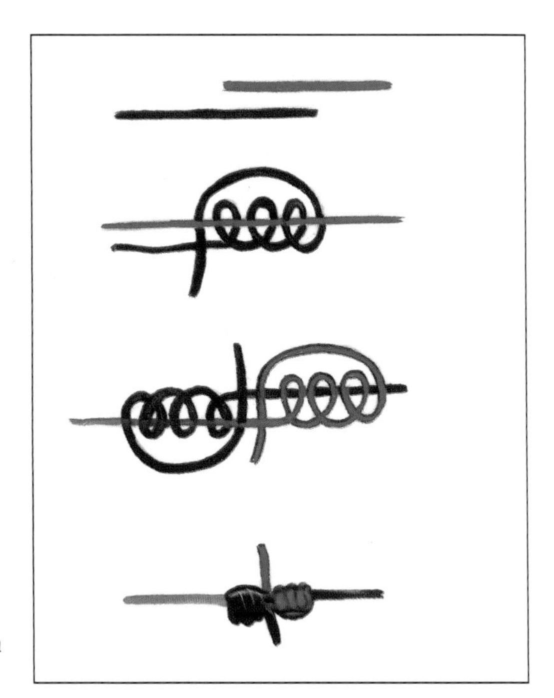

Three-turn Blood knot. For attaching nylon line to a leader.

Playing a Fish

Opinions differ on how to play a fish on fly tackle. One way is to give and take line with the spare hand rather than using the reel. Sometimes you must play fish this way, especially if a fish takes a lure at your feet when you have just retrieved a twenty-yard cast. If the fish is large enough it will run out the coils of fly line at your feet, but, if not, you may have problems in getting all the line back into your reel to play the fish in the normal way. Wherever possible I prefer to play the fish on the reel rather than hand play the fish with fly line.

Handling and Hook Removal

Always make sure your hands are wet before handling a fish. Grip the fish firmly but gently just behind the gill covers. If the hook is lightly embedded near the front of the mouth it is possible to remove it with the fingertips; otherwise, use a disgorger.

With larger fish, it is best to leave them lying in the damp net while you remove the hook. Artery forceps are best. When they are locked, a really good grip is maintained on the hook, which can be gently eased out. A damp towel positioned between the hand and the fish is advisable, as the larger fish are very strong and need some holding if they suddenly decide to leap about.

Retaining and Returning Fish

A large fish should be held underwater in an upright position with both hands until it swims away.

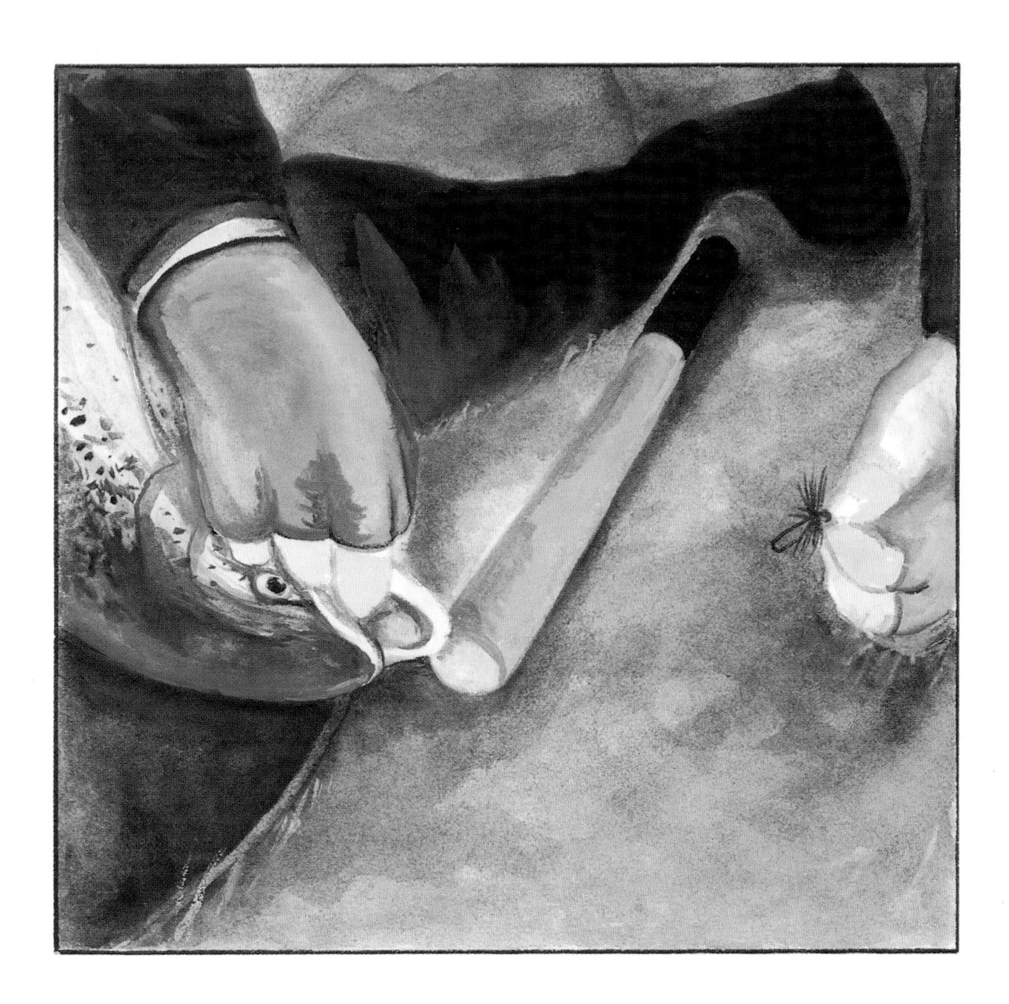

Index